Table of Contents

Are You Going to Eat That?

Imagine you are sitting at a table ready to enjoy a delicious dinner. The smell of food makes your stomach rumble. You can feel the heat coming off the plate. You pick up your fork. Carefully, you scoop the perfect bite. You slowly bring your fork to your mouth, ready for the first taste. As you take a closer look, you see little worms staring back at you. What do you do? Well, your reaction might not be the same as the person sitting next to you.

All over the world, people are eating certain bugs and **insects**. In fact, two billion people eat insects as part of their normal diet. In some places, insects are considered a dining **delicacy**. There are over 1,900 species of insects that are **edible**. The most common bugs that are eaten are beetles, caterpillars, bees, wasps, and ants. Some insects are raised on farms where they are cleaned, cooked, and prepared for packaging. Then, they are ready to be enjoyed as a tasty treat!

edible mealworms

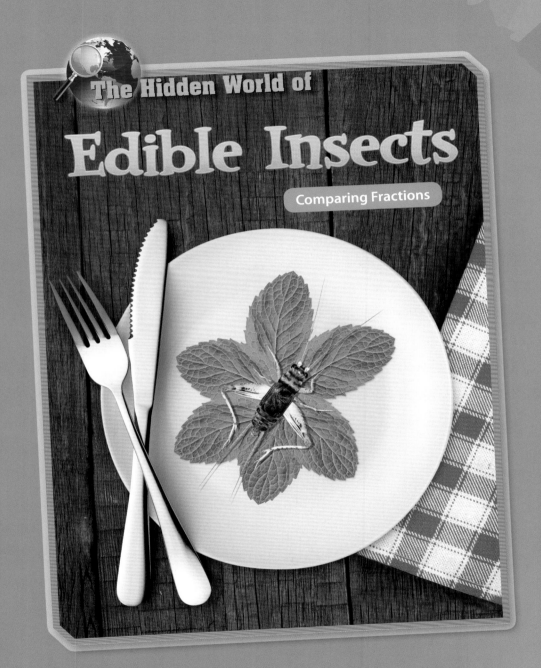

The Hidden World of

Edible Insects

Comparing Fractions

Molly Bibbo, M.A.T.

Consultants

Michele Ogden, Ed.D
Principal
Irvine Unified School District

Colleen Pollitt, M.A.Ed.
Math Support Teacher
Howard County Public Schools

Publishing Credits

Rachelle Cracchiolo, M.S.Ed., *Publisher*
Conni Medina, M.A.Ed., *Managing Editor*
Dona Herweck Rice, *Series Developer*
Emily R. Smith, M.A.Ed., *Series Developer*
Diana Kenney, M.A.Ed., NBCT, *Content Director*
Stacy Monsman, M.A., *Editor*
Kevin Panter, *Graphic Designer*

Image Credits: pp. 4–5 Luis Dafos/Alamy Stock Photo; pp. 8–9 meunierd/
Shutterstock, Inc.; p. 11 Mario Guzmán/EPA/Newscom; p. 13 Neil Setchfield/
Alamy Stock Photo;
p. 16 Cecil Bo Dzwowa/Shutterstock, Inc.; p. 18 (bottom), 20, 22 (bottom) 22–23
ton koene/Alamy Stock Photo; p. 19 (bottom) Jean-Christophe Verhaegen/
AFP/Getty Images; p. 24 (top and bottom) Mike Hutchings/Reuters; p. 27 (top)
Brent Lewin/Bloomberg via Getty Images; all other images from iStock and/or
Shutterstock.

Library of Congress Cataloging-in-Publication Data

Names: Bibbo, Molly Suzanne, author.
Title: The hidden world of edible insects / Molly Suzanne Bibbo, M.A.T.
Description: Huntington Beach, CA : Teacher Created Materials, [2017] |
    Audience: Grades 4-6. | Includes index.
Identifiers: LCCN 2017011895 (print) | LCCN 2017016388 (ebook) | ISBN
    9781480759350 (eBook) | ISBN 9781425855536 (pbk.)
Subjects: LCSH: Edible insects--Juvenile literature. | Food habits--Juvenile
    literature.
Classification: LCC TX746 (ebook) | LCC TX746 .B53 2017 (print) | DDC
    641.3/96--dc23
LC record available at https://lccn.loc.gov/2017011895

Teacher Created Materials

5301 Oceanus Drive
Huntington Beach, CA 92649-1030
http://www.tcmpub.com

ISBN 978-1-4258-5553-6
© 2018 Teacher Created Materials, Inc.
Printed by 51250
PO 10761 / Printed in USA

These fried scorpions are sold at street fairs in China.

Pests or Snacks?

People in different countries view insects in different ways. Some people think insects are pests, while others consider insects a snack or even a meal. The practice of eating insects, or **entomophagy**, is not new. People have been eating bugs for thousands of years.

For many years, and in many countries, people have found ways to make great tasting food with different types of bugs. Bugs can be made to taste sweet, salty, and even very spicy. Bees, beetles, spiders, and scorpions are just some of the critters that can make a delicious snack. How does a bowl of grasshoppers sound? How about fried worms? Well, don't knock them until you try them. More and more people are including insects in their daily diets. From Mexico to China, people are snacking on these crunchy insect treats.

fried bamboo worms with a chocolate-covered wafer bar

Mr. Ly surveys his fourth-grade students. He asks his class, "Would you eat a bug?" The results show that $\frac{1}{2}$ of his students would. Mr. Ly wants to rename the results two ways. Draw area models to show two fractions that are equivalent to $\frac{1}{2}$.

$$\frac{1}{2} = \frac{\square}{\square} = \frac{\square}{\square}$$

grasshoppers

fried silk worms

Treats from Thailand

A common snack in Thailand is called *Jing Leed*, also known as deep-fried crickets. These crunchy critters are cooked the same way as french fries. They are served with a salty sauce and sprinkled with white pepper.

People in Thailand also like to snack on silk worms. Silk worms are also fried, which makes them crunchy on the outside. The inside is a little softer, like mashed potatoes. But, when eating a silk worm, you don't bite it. Instead, you swallow it whole!

In Thailand, people can buy these delicious treats from vendors pushing carts on the street. All they have to do is choose the bugs they want to try and the size of the bag they want to buy. So, are you ready to swap a bag of your favorite potato chips for some crispy crickets or salty silk worms?

LET'S EXPLORE MATH

Imagine that you buy a bag of silk worms that weighs $\frac{1}{3}$ pound. How can this fraction be renamed as an equivalent fraction in sixths? Draw and label the number lines to show your solution.

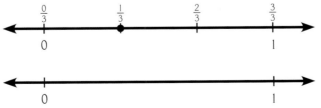

Delicacies of Mexico

Mexico has the highest number of edible insects in the world. It has over 300 types to choose from. Most of them are caught in the wild. Some of the more popular delicacies are ant **larvae**, water bug eggs, and stinkbugs. Stinkbugs, or *jumiles*, get their name from the smelly odor they give off when they feel threatened. In Mexico, people put jumiles in tacos. They taste like cinnamon and mint. Sometimes, when people eat them, the bugs are still alive!

After enjoying a jumiles taco, it's time to top it off with a sweet treat. A popular dessert in Mexico is a **locust** dipped in warm chocolate. A locust is a large, green insect. It looks like a grasshopper.

Another big hit are bug lollipops, or *chupetes*. The candy comes in different colors and flavors. You must lick the lollipop to get to the best part— the bug!

cricket lollipop

jumiles taco

Suppose you want to buy chocolate-covered locusts and notice that the bigger the locust, the higher the price. A small locust costs $\frac{1}{2}$ of a dollar. A large locust costs $\frac{8}{10}$ of a dollar. Which of the following fractions of a dollar make sense as possible costs for a medium locust? Explain your reasoning.

A. $\frac{2}{4}$

B. $\frac{1}{6}$

C. $\frac{3}{5}$

D. $\frac{3}{4}$

E. $\frac{9}{10}$

F. $\frac{1}{3}$

Fried scorpions are served on skewers in China.

fried silk worm larvae

12

Snacks from China

People in China eat a variety of bugs. One popular snack is fried scorpions. Scorpions may look scary with their stingers and claws. But, this does not stop people from eating them. These large, fierce bugs are cooked to a crisp. (Once grilled or fried, they are no longer poisonous.)

You can order two types of scorpion skewers in China—large (adults) or small (babies). Some people like to eat scorpions that are still alive. They think eating live scorpions helps to cure a number of medical conditions.

If a scorpion on a stick doesn't sound **appetizing**, there are plenty of other choices. You could try a centipede on a stick. Maybe a spider skewer is your style. You could also try roasted bee larvae or fried silk worm larvae. Or, you might prefer a hot, steamy bowl of ant soup. Do any of those sound tasty to you?

fried centipede on a stick

13

Why Eat Insects?

So, are you ready to trade your slice of cake for a chocolate locust? What about a bag of potato chips for some crunchy crickets? Not quite? Well, perhaps it's important to learn *why* people choose insects as appetizers.

fried mealworms

How Do They Taste?

On the outside, bugs may look pretty gross. However, some experts say that bugs are more appetizing than they may look. Dr. Bill White is an **entomologist** who works in Louisiana. He is an insect expert. He traveled to Thailand to do some research. While he was there, he ate large water bugs and roasted mealworms. He really enjoyed the mealworms. When asked how the bugs taste, Dr. White said that they are crispy and have a nutty flavor. This seems to be the usual reaction from people.

Some bugs, like bee larvae, are said to have a sweet taste. Many people in East Asia enjoy eating bee larvae for that reason. The baby bees look like small, chubby worms and are cooked and served as a juicy indulgence.

fried crickets

LET'S EXPLORE MATH

Dr. White likes the taste of the mealworms so much that he wants to fry some for dinner. He uses a recipe that calls for $\frac{3}{4}$-cup mealworms per serving. He only has a $\frac{1}{8}$-measuring cup.

How can Dr. White use this measuring cup to make one serving? Explain your reasoning.

A boy eats dried, protein-rich termites, which are delicacies in some African countries.

A Good Source of Protein

Another reason that many people snack on insects is because they are a good source of **protein**. Muscles and organs need protein to make new cells. Protein gives your body the energy it needs to move, grow, and build muscle.

Most of the protein people eat comes from meat. Pigs, chicken, fish, and cows are great sources of protein. Bugs are packed with protein, too. Some bugs have more protein than others. The bugs with the most protein are flies, termites, and rice grasshoppers. Snacking on a handful of these critters can give people the energy and strength they need. Some people might think it's a much healthier choice than a bag of chips or a candy bar!

fried grasshopper

Other Health Benefits

Besides protein, bugs are a great source of **calcium**. Bones need calcium to stay strong. People can get calcium by drinking milk or eating cheese.

It turns out that crickets are also full of calcium. About four crickets have as much calcium as a glass of milk! Cooked crickets can be ground into a powder to make pasta or flour. Cricket flour can be used to bake a cake. Or, it can be mixed with water or juice to make a healthy drink.

Insects are packed with many other nutrients that human bodies need to stay healthy and strong. Insects can be a source of fiber and iron. These nutrients keep your body working the way it should and help you feel great. And, insects are said to fight off sickness. The next time you feel tired and need a boost, a toasted caterpillar might be the cure you need!

edible worm treat from Holland

fried crickets

A factory worker in France prepares pasta made from cricket and locust flour.

A bug farmer in Holland cares for edible insects.

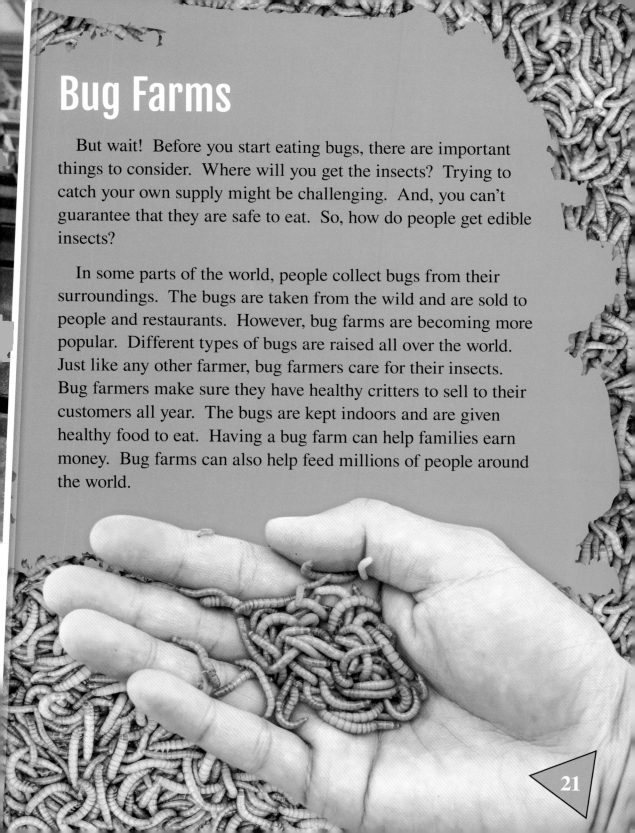

Bug Farms

But wait! Before you start eating bugs, there are important things to consider. Where will you get the insects? Trying to catch your own supply might be challenging. And, you can't guarantee that they are safe to eat. So, how do people get edible insects?

In some parts of the world, people collect bugs from their surroundings. The bugs are taken from the wild and are sold to people and restaurants. However, bug farms are becoming more popular. Different types of bugs are raised all over the world. Just like any other farmer, bug farmers care for their insects. Bug farmers make sure they have healthy critters to sell to their customers all year. The bugs are kept indoors and are given healthy food to eat. Having a bug farm can help families earn money. Bug farms can also help feed millions of people around the world.

Cricket Farms

A common insect that you might find on a bug farm is a cricket. A cricket farm is much smaller than a cattle farm. In fact, a cricket farm can be made with just a few large boxes or containers. Although these farms are small, they can produce tons of crickets. A single container can hold up to 500 crickets! And, most farms have hundreds of containers.

Just like cattle farmers, cricket farmers must give their bugs food and water. Luckily, crickets do not eat very much, and they grow very fast. It only takes about a month for crickets to grow. When crickets are ready to be sold, farmers freeze them. This helps crickets **hibernate**. Then, they can be roasted and sold whole. Or, they can be ground into a fine powder and sold as cricket flour.

cricket farm

Mr. Somwan has a cricket farm in Thailand. He can only sell crickets that weigh at least $\frac{1}{4}$ gram. Which of the following are weights of crickets that can be sold? Explain your reasoning.

A. $\frac{1}{8}$ g   **C.** $\frac{3}{5}$ g   **E.** $\frac{2}{8}$ g

B. $\frac{1}{2}$ g   **D.** $\frac{1}{3}$ g   **F.** $\frac{2}{12}$ g

Workers move a container of rotting vegetables to feed fly larvae.

A visitor to the world's largest fly farm stands behind an enclosure of flies.

Fly Farms

Crickets are not the only insects raised by farmers. Other bugs you may find on a bug farm are flies. Flies start their lives as **maggots**, which look like plump little worms. Like crickets, maggots are packed with protein and are very easy to care for. And, they do not take up much space. A fly farm can hold billions of insects.

The largest fly farm in the world is near Cape Town, South Africa. The farm has over eight billion maggots and flies. The flies are only fed food that people have thrown away. This helps eliminate extra waste. Unlike cricket farms, maggots and flies at this farm are not raised to feed people. This fly farm makes food for animals, such as cows.

maggots

Good for You and Good for the Planet

There are a lot of people living on our planet. In fact, Earth's **population** totals about seven billion. Raising enough cows and chickens to feed everyone in the world is a challenge. Animals need lots of space, food, and water to grow. And, feeding large animals can be very **expensive**.

Millions of people around the world are crunching on critters. Not only are bugs tasty, they are packed with nutrients that can keep people strong and healthy. Most importantly, bugs can help feed a lot of people in the world for a lot less money.

So, next time you eat a salad, do you dare to sprinkle some toasted crickets on top? Or, will you use cricket flour to bake your next cake? If the answer is no, don't worry. The idea of eating bugs may take some getting used to!

A man in Cambodia eats a fried tarantula, which is thought to cure breathing problems and backaches.

🛠️ Problem Solving

Would you like to sink your teeth into a warm chocolate chip cookie? How about one with a mealworm surprise? Look at the ingredients for Mealworm Chocolate Chip Cookies. Then, answer the questions.

1. The recipe calls for $\frac{2}{3}$ cup of ground mealworms. Imagine you only have a $\frac{1}{6}$-measuring cup. How can you use this cup to measure the correct amount of mealworms? Draw area models to prove your solution.

2. You will need $\frac{3}{4}$ cup of butter for this recipe. Rename $\frac{3}{4}$ as an equivalent fraction in eighths. Draw number lines to show your thinking.

3. Suppose you only have a $\frac{1}{4}$-measuring cup. How many scoops of chocolate chips will you need?

4. Will you need more white sugar or brown sugar? How do you know?

5. Does the recipe call for a greater amount of brown sugar, flour, or ground mealworms? Order the amounts from greatest to least to show your thinking.

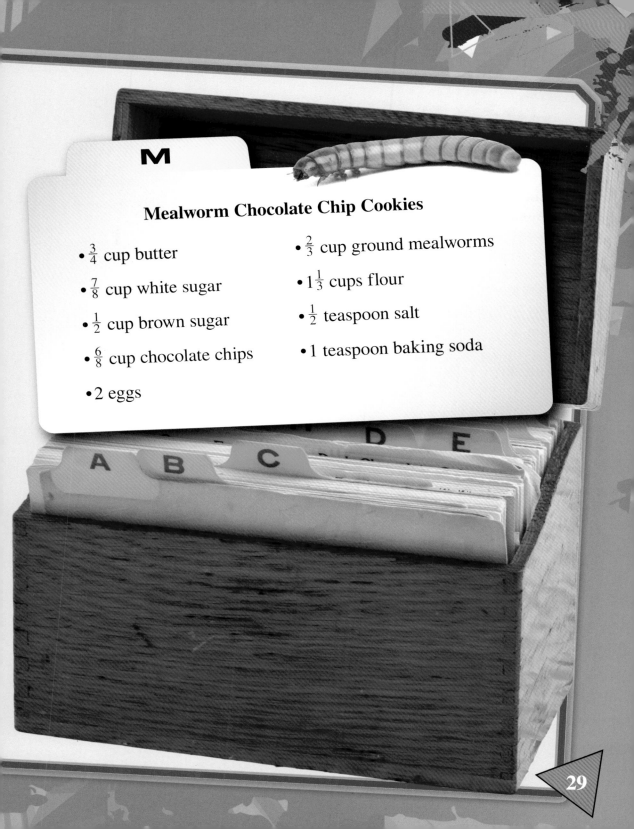

Mealworm Chocolate Chip Cookies

- $\frac{3}{4}$ cup butter
- $\frac{7}{8}$ cup white sugar
- $\frac{1}{2}$ cup brown sugar
- $\frac{6}{8}$ cup chocolate chips
- 2 eggs

- $\frac{2}{3}$ cup ground mealworms
- $1\frac{1}{3}$ cups flour
- $\frac{1}{2}$ teaspoon salt
- 1 teaspoon baking soda

Glossary

appetizing—having a pleasant smell or appearance that makes it good to eat

calcium—mineral that makes bones strong

delicacy—something enjoyable to eat but rare to find

edible—safe to eat

entomologist—a scientist who studies insects

entomophagy—the practice of eating insects for food

expensive—costing a lot of money

hibernate—to sleep or rest in the winter

insects—small animals with six legs and wings

larvae—young insects that look like worms

locust—a type of grasshopper

maggots—young flies that look like worms

population—a group of people or animals living in the same place

protein—a nutrient found in foods, such as meat, milk, eggs, and beans

Index

Answer Key

Let's Explore Math

page 7:

Answers will vary. Possible answer: $\frac{1}{2} = \frac{2}{4} = \frac{4}{8}$; Area models should all show $\frac{1}{2}$ of the model shaded.

page 9:

$\frac{1}{3} = \frac{2}{6}$; Number line should be partitioned into 6 equal parts with a point plotted at $\frac{2}{6}$.

page 11:

Choices C and D are correct because both $\frac{3}{5}$ and $\frac{3}{4}$ are greater than $\frac{1}{2}$ but less than $\frac{8}{10}$.

page 15:

Explanations will vary, but should include that the $\frac{1}{8}$-cup measuring cup can be scooped 6 times to make $\frac{6}{8}$ or $\frac{3}{4}$ cup of mealworms.

page 23:

Choices B, C, D, and E are correct because they are equivalent to or greater than $\frac{1}{4}$.

Problem Solving

1. $\frac{2}{3} = \frac{4}{6}$; One area model should show 2 parts shaded out of 3 equal parts. The second area model should show 4 parts shaded out of 6 equal parts.

2. $\frac{3}{4} = \frac{6}{8}$; Number lines should show points labeled $\frac{3}{4}$ and $\frac{6}{8}$ plotted in the same location.

3. 3 scoops; $\frac{1}{4} = \frac{2}{8}$; $\frac{3}{4} = \frac{6}{8}$

4. white sugar; $\frac{7}{8} > \frac{1}{2}$ or $\frac{4}{8}$

5. flour; $1\frac{1}{3}$ (flour), $\frac{2}{3}$ (ground mealworms), $\frac{1}{2}$ (brown sugar)